Redesign Your Mind

The Hidden Power of Haiku

Bridget Baker

Text copyrighted © 2017 by Bridget Baker
All rights reserved

No part of this book may be reproduced, or stored in a retrieval system, or transmitted in any form, or by any means, electronic, mechanical, photocopying, recording or otherwise, without express written permission of the publisher.

ISBN 9781520966175

Cover art by Bridget Baker
Copy Edited by Andrea Baker

DEDICATION

For Andrea, who was, and is, my inspiration

TABLE OF CONTENTS

INTRODUCTION.....1

Section I – Length and Form.....8

Rule 1: Use 17 syllables or less

Rule 2: Arrange on three lines

Rule 3: Should not read as a sentence

Rule 4: Avoid stops at the end of each line

Rule 5: Do not use a title

Section II – Language and Punctuation.....15

Rule 6: Avoid rhyming

Rule 7: Only capitalize proper nouns

Rule 8: Use little or no punctuation

Rule 9: Use commonplace words

Rule 10: Avoid repeated words

Section III – Subject Matter

Rule 11: Tranquil, uplifting subject matter

Rule 12: Avoid human intervention

Rule 13: Use a seasonal word

Rule 14: Use concrete images

Rule 15: Keep it real and immediate

Section IV – Viewpoint…..29

Rule 16: Avoid judgments

Rule 17: Do not try to convey a message

Rule 18: Avoid negativity

Rule 19: Avoid being too sweet

Rule 20: Do not Humanize Non-human Elements

Rule 21: Clichés, Metaphors and Similes

Section V–Grammatical Conventions…..43

Rule 22: Stay in the present tense

Rule 23: Limits for nouns and verbs

Rule 24: End with a noun

Rule 25: Use singular forms

Rule 26: Avoid personal pronouns

Putting it into Practice…..58

Practical Exercises

Summing it All Up…..8586

INTRODUCTION

The process of finding serenity through haiku is as short and simple as haiku itself. For those of you not familiar with the Japanese form of poetry known as haiku, it is a tiny narrative that does not rhyme and is no longer than 17 syllables in length.

The majority of us could use a little more serenity in our lives. One of the reasons that stress has replaced tranquility for the average person is that urban living has taken us so far away from the natural world. When this happens, there is a tendency to switch our natural rhythms with the hurried, artificial pace of human creations, like commuter traffic or the marketplace. This is not the way we were intended to live, and the result is stress, tension, and potentially disease.

Haiku is the polar opposite of this pressure and tension that makes up so much of our daily lives. Haiku is a tightly condensed form of Japanese poetry containing just 17 syllables, which tells a brief story that paints an evocative picture. It is then up to the reader to draw out the meanings from the haiku and in doing so, the reader is compelled to block out all of the chaos and confusion that are competing for his or her attention.

One of the primary objectives of haiku is to create a calming, tranquil mood. When we can focus on simply what is before us, we are what eastern philosophers refer to as "being in the moment." If we are being in the moment, we are not worrying about the future or having regrets about the past – which are two things that we cannot change. Worrying about things we cannot change is one of the primary causes of stress.

Haiku is an art form that can put you back in touch with the tranquil rhythms that nature created for you. It can clear your mind and make it easy for you live in the present instead of trying to be three places at once – the past, the present and the future. Writing haiku involves reducing what you observe down to the just the bare essentials and then creating a relationship between the elements that will make the reader's mind leap between them. We live in a holographic universe, and the whole is reflected in each and every part – no matter how small.

This uncomplicated form of poetry has been imported to English-speaking countries with a few variations. The simplicity of haiku – [pronounced: high-**coo**] – produces a calming and uplifting effect.If you are willing to spend a few minutes a day writing haiku for the next 21 to 30 days (approximately the time it takes to form a new habit) you will find yourself – among other things:

- More serene
- Less stressed
- Smiling more
- More observant

- Less judgmental
- More accepting (and hence more accepted)
- A more effective speaker
- Closer to nature
- More organized
- Less forgetful
- More decisive
- Carrying less clutter and holding fewer grudges

If you are willing to perform the exercise of writing a little haiku each day, you will begin to change the way you look at the world, the way you think about things, as well as the way you react to what used to be stressful situations. When you change your perception of the world around you, you will literally change your life. You may be surprised at how far this subtle shift in thinking will go towards turning you into the type of person who sails serenely through life, rising easily to whatever challenges you may encounter.

CAN YOU HAIKU?

You may not think you can write haiku, but I'm going to walk you through it step by step and you will quickly realize that you can. You always have the option of honing your craft further, but just the basic steps will be enough to change the way you form your thoughts and help you see how this will allow you to you reach the inner peace that will make life flow smoothly.

Traditional haiku will most often have a seasonal tie-in which acts as a symbol, i.e. Spring denotes youth and new beginnings while Autumn might convey melancholy, advancing age and reflections of life that is winding down. To illustrate, I have reprinted the following poem written Matsuo Basho [1644-1694] who is considered one of the masters of this form.

along this road

that no one else travels

autumn nightfall

Because this was written in Japanese and translated into English, the syllable count may not come as expected. However as you read the poem, you can see how simple haiku is.

This tiny little form of poetry carries quite a few conventions in addition to the syllable count.

Once you know these conventions, you can abide by or ignore as many as you like, following just enough of the rules to make your poem recognizable as haiku. The purpose of doing the exercises in this book is to achieve an inner serenity; therefore we will be concentrating primarily on those conventions that will lead us to that place.

When reading haiku for the first time many people have the same reaction they had the first time they saw an exhibit of modern art – "I can do that!" This is absolutely the right reaction - you *can* do it! One of the conventions is that you write only what you know or see in front of you. Other conventions are that you use only ordinary words and little or no punctuation. Haiku guidelines also stipulate that you do not rhyme and that your finished poem should not present a message, philosophy or judgment. Putting your observations into a ku (meaning a haiku poem) of 17 syllables forces you to drop judgments and see only what is there – you are forced to live in the present (stay in the moment) not drifting into the past (regrets) or future (fear).

So as you can see, the many conventions of haiku make it simple, not difficult.

- Keep it short
- No rhyming
- No punctuation
- Use ordinary words
- No message or philosophy
- Write what you know about

What could be easier? Here we have half a dozen rules that basically boil down to one message – keep it simple. So keep this in mind as you move into the later chapters and begin to look at some more guidelines and learn how adopting these guidelines in your writing can bring you peace of mind. It is more important to be true to yourself than to be "correct" by the rules.

In the chapters that follow you will learn some of the guidelines for writing haiku – what makes it different from other forms of poetry. The majority of the conventions or guidelines we are going to work with encourage you to keep it simple. Many of them are merely telling you what you *don't* have to do. Besides keeping it short and simple, you can forget about rhyming, punctuation, capitalization, a title and about imparting any message or philosophy.

You will find as many lists of rules as you will find haiku experts and you will even find some rules that contradict one another. Basho – one of the recognized masters of haiku – says "learn the rules, and then forget them". This means that once you truly understand what is (and what is not) haiku, you are free to break any of the rules when you are writing your own poetry as long as you follow enough of the guidelines to make your work recognizable as haiku.

To get to that place though, you will need to follow the conventions as closely as possible while you are learning. Some of the guidelines are more important than others, and I will be listing the conventions roughly in order of importance. First, those guidelines that will create poems that qualify as haiku, and then those guidelines which are most important to achieving the Zen state of tranquility that we are working towards.

As you practice applying these guidelines to your compositions, you will come to think of most guidelines as boundaries rather than limitations. By the end of these exercises, you will have developed a style all of your own within the group of guidelines with which you resonate most strongly. At that point you will have become a true artist.

This book is presented in 5 sections – each containing exercises to build the skills and understanding you need for the next section. Along the way, you will discover what you can expect to gain from integrating these skills. At the end of the book there is a group of daily exercises. By working through one of these each day, you will learn to write good haiku easily and effortlessly and as you do, you will start to notice your stress falling away. As you begin dropping your judgments and living in the present, it will become easier and easier to achieve the serenity that can sometimes feel so elusive.

Section I – Length and Form

In this first section you will learn the basic guidelines for writing haiku. The primary conventions that set haiku apart from other forms of poetry are:

- Use 17 syllables or less
- Arrange on three lines
- Should not read as a sentence
- Avoid stops after each line
- Do not use a title

I am going to use an example from an English language haiku as we go over these first five guidelines. If you have already written some haiku of your own, you can edit your own work as we look at these guidelines. If you wish you did have some examples of your own, feel free to jump ahead to the exercises in the final section and start writing. Reworking your own writing is the best way to truly grasp how the techniques we are discussing will make your work stronger and alter your perception to create the serenity we want to achieve.

EXAMPLE FOR SECTION I

THE VULTURE

BIG AND BLACK AND STRONG AM I.

I WAIT UNTIL THE OXEN DIE,

THEN EAT.

Let's compare the example above to each of the guidelines in this section to see how it stacks up.

Rule 1: Use 17 syllables or less

You are always going to find disagreement among purists when you are discussing the guidelines for haiku, but that should just reassure you that there is plenty of room for individual differences. Some of the guidelines are interpreted in different ways due to the changes that occur when haiku moves from the native Japanese into the English language. For example, there is much more information in 17 English syllables than in the same number of Japanese syllables.

For this reason many writers believe that an English language haiku should have fewer syllables to achieve the same discipline and economy. I for one tend to agree with that in most cases, and you should feel free use less syllables if you feel the same or if you would have to add unnecessary words to bring your poem up to 17 syllables For our purposes here, we will simply use 17 syllables as our upper limit – you can use less if you like, but not more.

In our example here, the syllable count is exactly 17. Sometimes this happens naturally, and sometimes it shows where the author has done some padding (or trimming) to make the count come out a certain way. Remember, 17 syllables is an upper limit. Never use unnecessary words just to pad the syllable count.

As you go through this book and perform the exercises, you will develop the habit of conveying your message in as few words as possible. In daily life, you will seldom be limited to 17 syllables, but the disciplines you develop writing haiku help you to stay focused and eliminate unnecessary fillers in your writing and speaking.

PRACTICAL EXERCISE

Think of something that brings a smile to your face and write a short paragraph describing it. Now focus on one small detail of this story and reduce it to a haiku using no more than 17 syllables.

First tell your story. *Example:* I saw a mother rabbit and her baby hopping out of an iris patch my way to the bus stop this morning. Their fluffy white tails were so cute! I startled them and they hopped off quickly. Then I noticed they went off in two directions to make it harder for a predator to catch them both.

Then narrow your story down to one detail in time or space. *Example:* Two rabbits with white tails hopped off in separate directions as I approached.

And lastly, focus this observation into a narrative of 17 syllables or less.

EXAMPLE:

two downy white tails
small disappeared to the right
large one vanished left

Now make up your own story and use the three-step process above to create your own haiku. This exercise will help you focus on the present moment without any judgements.

Rule 2: Arrange on three lines

Your haiku should be divided into two parts. Each smaller part [five syllables] is called a fragment and the longer [seven syllable] part is called a phrase. Use few, if any, articles such as "an" "a" or "the", in the fragment, but the phrase should read like correct English. Although most haiku are written with the syllables divided as 5/7/5, it can also be written and 5/12 or 12/5 syllables. This is variation is often used if your haiku makes a riddle.

Lines one and three should be connected or related in some way. Traditional ways to connect these would be either to compare or contrast your subject matter. For example; near and far, or young and old, or perhaps abundant and sparse. This structure will add some mystery and intrigue to your poetry, making it the kind of haiku that your audience will read more than once. We will expand on this idea as we progress through the guidelines.

The haiku in our example is written in three lines, and the divisions seem natural and smooth.

Rule 3: Should not read as a sentence

Haiku is a form of poetry and it has an arrangement of its own unrelated to the sentence structure of prose. If you write a single sentence, it will not have the poetic beauty of haiku and you will simply be making a statement rather than creating a narrative that makes the readers' minds make a leap. Make sure that your haiku does not read as a run-on sentence separated by grammar or punctuation.
Take another look at the example for this section to help us understand this guideline:

The Vulture
Big and black and strong am I.
I wait until the oxen die,
Then eat.

This example would be considered a "run-on sentence" because of the way you can read all three lines together as one sentence. Read this out loud and notice how you can read all three lines as a single thought, or statement.

Big and black and strong am I, I wait until the oxen die, then eat.

PRACTICAL EXERCISE

Read the following two examples several times to get a feel for the difference it makes when the same story is told in the form of a sentence or in the form of haiku.

EXAMPLE:

diamond-like dewdrops
will disappear completely
when the sun rises

EXAMPLE AFTER EDITING:

garden at daybreak
sun's rays warm the morning air
diamonds disappear

I've given an example below which also could be read as a run-on sentence. For this exercise, use the example as a starting point and re-write it so that it so that it does not read as a sentence. Feel free to substitute words and phrases of your own to tell the same story. Try to incorporate the other guidelines we have learned – 17 syllable maximum, arrange on three lines – but concentrate primarily on the new guideline we are learning and make the narrative below sound less like a sentence.

PRACTICAL EXERCISE

rioting daffodils everywhere
spread rumors of
summer's return

Rule 4: Avoid stops at the end of each line

Example:
Big and black and strong am I. [Period]
I wait until the oxen die. [Period]
Then eat. [Period]

The author has created a very choppy haiku. Notice how the poem gives you a tendency to stop or pause at the end of each line almost as though there were a period. You may find this easier to notice if you read the poem out loud.
Stops at the end of line can be created either by punctuation or by the grammar and phrasing that is used by the author. The reader will stop both when the punctuation gives an instruction to stop (like a period, comma or colon) and when the way the words are used make it seem natural to stop.

Rule 5: Do not use a title

Obviously our example does not follow this guideline. The title in this case is also acting as another line which puts this haiku over the 17 syllable limit. So let's put the information that we find in the title into the poem and remove some of the unnecessary words to stay below the 17 syllable limit and see what happens.

The vulture is black and strong
He waits until the oxen die
To eat

Notice that we still have 17 syllables. Now let's see how our example stacks up against the next set of guidelines.

These are the basics; now let's move on to the next set of guidelines.

Section II – Language and Punctuation

- Avoid rhyming
- Use capital letters only on proper nouns
- Use little or no punctuation
- Use commonplace words
- Avoid repeated or unnecessary words

Rule 6: Avoid rhyming

Rhyming is easy and monotonous and will only detract from the feeling you want to convey. The haiku in our next example rhymes the first and second line. This can be very distracting in a poetry form that is this short, and may divert the reader from what the writer is trying to say.

Example:

<u>The Vulture</u>
Big and black and strong am I.
I wait until the oxen die,
Then eat.

As we look closely at the haiku, we can see how awkward the first sentence is because of the author's attempt to make a rhyme. We can correct both problems at one time by re-writing the haiku to read:

I'm big, black and strong
I wait until the oxen die
Then eat

Rule 7: Only capitalize proper nouns

When we made the changes above, we eliminated two of the three problems here, because of course the 'I' would still be capitalized. To conform to the guidelines we simply change the example to:

I'm big, black and strong
I wait until the oxen die
then eat

Rule 8: Use little or no punctuation

From the original example, we would remove the periods and commas from the end of each line. The phrasing of the haiku alone tells the reader when to pause and no punctuation is necessary.

Rule 9: Use commonplace words

Use ordinary words – your reader should never need to reach for a dictionary. This guideline forces you to pay attention to the subtle differences between words, which will improve your vocabulary in the long run. When you are working with just 17 syllables, every word has to count so choose words with complex connotations. In haiku, adverbs and adjectives are also minimized, so it is critical to use exactly the right noun or verb if you want the reader to understand what you are saying. As you search for exactly the right word to get your meaning across you will come to appreciate the nuances between the multitudes of words that mean basically the same thing. For example, if you are writing about a leaf falling off a tree, notice the difference between the mental images you get when you substitute the following words for the original verb.

I watched a leaf *fall* from the tree.

Or
I watched a leaf *plunge* from the tree.

Or
I watched a leaf *tumble* from the tree.

Or
I watched a leaf *drift* down from the tree.

These examples hold up well. These are all words people use in everyday conversation and no reader would need a dictionary and they are words heavy with connotations.

Rule 10: Avoid repeated words

Using a phrase like "ruby red petals" would be an example of repeated words. Even though they are actually different words, they both convey the same meaning. See how much more poetic it sounds when you simply say "ruby petals". An example of unnecessary words would be a phrase like "young puppy". By calling this dog a puppy, you would have already said that it is young.

In the original example, 'and' was repeated as well as the word 'I' and in our re-written haiku, the word 'I' is still repeated. Although the words 'big' and 'strong' have different meanings, there is nothing added to this haiku by using both words. In a borderline situation like this, remember that we want to use a minimum number of words – so if the word adds nothing to the story, the general guideline would be to eliminate it.

Let's see what we can do to bring this haiku more in line with the guidelines we have covered so far.

EXAMPLE FOR SECTION I

black vulture
waits until the oxen die
then eats

Or

strong vulture
waits until the oxen die
then eats

Somehow neither version paints the same picture as the version beginning "strong, black vulture". We have two choices in a situation like this – we can either come up with a word that conveys the meaning of both of the words (strong and black) or we can eliminate both of them.

Since it is your own work you are going to be editing in these exercises, you are always going to know what the author meant – what story needs to be conveyed. In our example, the author wanted to convey a sense of foreboding. To this author, a vulture is ominous, threatening or menacing. If you stop to think about it, the very word "vulture" conveys any and all of those meanings by itself, so we can safely eliminate both adjectives without losing any meaning. This will keep the haiku light and tight by eliminating unnecessary words.

Our final version then reads:
a vulture
waits until the oxen die
then eats

Now compare this to the version of this example we started with.

The Vulture
Big and black and strong am I.
I wait until the oxen die,
Then eat.

Read the new version out loud a few times. Can you hear how much stronger it is? To review what we have done so far, here is the list of guidelines for form and structure. Use this list to critique our example and/or your own work.

- Use 17 syllables or less
- Arrange on three lines
- Should not read as a sentence
- Avoid stops after each line
- Do not use a title
- Avoid rhyming
- Use capital letters only when using proper nouns
- Use little or no punctuation
- Use commonplace words
- Avoid repeated or unnecessary words

The form and length fit the guidelines, but we had to remove the title. Then we added the information in the title to the existing haiku, and changed the wording to accommodate this addition. Next, we removed the rhyme in the first and second lines. We then removed the unnecessary capital letters, and removed the punctuation. As the final step, we removed the repeated words leaving us the haiku below:

a vulture
waits until the oxen die
then eats

While we were doing through the required steps to edit this example down to the final version, your subconscious mind was learning to think in a new way. You began to think more concisely, and eliminate anything unnecessary thereby allowing the words to carry the meaning, not artificial sign posts like punctuation.

Quite a difference – shall we take our haiku to the next level?

Section III – Subject Matter

- Tranquil, uplifting subject matter
- Reflect on nature without human intervention
- Use a seasonal word
- Use concrete images, not abstract thoughts
- Subject matter should be real and immediate

One of the objectives of haiku is to create a calm, quiet mood by choosing our subject matter carefully and presently it thoughtfully. When you are able to incorporate all, or most of the guidelines in this section, you will easily create the mood we are looking for.

EXAMPLE:
a vulture
waits until the oxen die
then eats

We all know that oxen will eventually die and vultures need to eat – but this topic most definitely does not pass our first guideline regarding subject matter. It is absolutely *not* going to create the calm, quiet mood that we want to transmit with haiku. Let's begin with a new example – one that already incorporates the guidelines we have been working with.

EXAMPLE:
pleasure remembered
mother let us stay up late
catching fireflies

Much better subject matter! Let's do a quick review here of the guidelines we've already covered. This example has no title, no rhyming, no punctuation, and no capital letters. It uses commonplace words and none are repeated. We have 17 syllables on three lines that are not chopped up by stops at the end of each line and do not read as a run-on sentence. Everything looks great so far. Now let's take a look at the next set of guidelines to see how we can bring our haiku to the next level.

Rule 11: Tranquil, uplifting subject matter

This does not mean that we are looking for playful waves, sun-kissed butterflies or purple mountains majesty. The general guideline is to avoid topics like war, violence, crime, disease or explicit sex. Haiku is about the little things in life, like the sun shining through the delicate leaves of a sycamore or a single drop of morning dew.

It can even be about things like a rusty mail box if the poet uses the right word images to make us think about some wonderful moments that the owner experienced as a result of receiving letters from loved ones or simply appreciating how this old mail box has been their link with the outside world over the years. Fireflies on late warm summer evenings have certainly brought joy to more than one reader – our new example fits this guideline nicely.

Rule 12: Avoid human intervention

EXAMPLE:

pleasure remembered
mother let us stay up late
catching fireflies

This haiku is definitely about nature, however, when the author introduced the word "mother", the element of human intervention entered this haiku. It is a simple matter to edit it out without changing the meaning.

pleasure remembered
staying up late
catching fireflies

Can you feel the difference? Now anyone can read the haiku and feel what the author felt - it does not matter if the reader had a mother, or if the mother was the one who gave permission to stay up late - or even if the reader *had* permission to stay up late! The reader could even "be" the mother and get the same feeling of a pleasant summer evening. The more we eliminate, the more people can relate to the haiku.

Rule 13: Use a seasonal word

Not every haiku will incorporate a seasonal word, but establishing a season in your haiku does several things because of the natural associations we have when we think about a season. Traditionally, spring is associated with hope, rebirth and new life, while summer brings to mind fullness, reaching adulthood and the freedom of vacation time. It is natural to associate autumn with not only the abundance of the harvest season, but also with the touch of melancholy we get from things coming to an end. It is a time of maturity that causes us to realize that our productive years are coming to an end. Wintertime is traditionally associated with rest, nighttime and old age.

When you introduce a seasonal word into your haiku you will also establish a stage of life or a phase of development such as the beginning of a relationship (spring) that progresses to the commitment of marriage (summer) and the feeling of satisfaction and accomplishment that comes from raising a family and building a home (fall) then ends through separation or death (winter). Using a time of day in your haiku (without naming it) will accomplish the same thing.

This is a guideline that may require a little practice to implement smoothly. However, once you get in the habit of finding a way to convey the season with a single word or short phrase that brings the season to mind, you will make great strides towards changing the way your mind works. This is one of the ways that a good haiku gives the mind some exercise both when you are reading it and when you are writing it.

A seasonal word for winter might be "snowflake". If the writer wanted the reader to think about springtime, words like "daffodil" or "apple blossoms" would do the trick. Notice how the words "bonfire" and "golden leaves" make you automatically think of fall. Do you have any trouble figuring out what season the poem in our example is referring to? Probably not – and the reason is that almost everyone naturally associates fireflies with summer. So in this haiku, the kigo, or seasonal word is "fireflies."

Experiment with this for yourself by labeling four pages of paper with the names of the seasons. These pages can form the beginning of your own personal haiku journal where you can keep a record of your progress and include your own versions of our exercise as well as any notes you want to make.

Start a list on each one of words that represent the season for that page. Add to the lists as you think of more words. Adding to the lists is a great way to overcome any blocks you may encounter during the practical exercises. In the beginning your lists might look something like this:

Spring:
Dogwood trees
Thawing
Melting
Apple blossoms
Wind
Birds
Daffodils
Buds
Newborns (calf, kitten, puppy, etc).

Summer:
Bees
Sailboats
Lawnmower noises
Green grass
Shade trees
Popsicles
Hot sun
Tanning lotion (smell)
Vacation

Fall:
Golden leaves
Wood smoke
Raked leaves
Migrating birds
Geese (sound)
Crisp mornings
Bonfires
Pumpkins
Harvest

Winter
Snowflakes
Early darkness
Skating (activity)
Mittens
Snowdrifts
Bare branches
Frost
Icicles

You will find that a season can be brought to mind by any one of the five senses; a sight, a sound, a smell, a taste or a touch and even by an activity or a time of day.

Rule 14: Use concrete images

In haiku, we are simply observing nature and reporting what we see. It is up to the reader to decide what he or she thinks about what we are reporting. The haiku in our example has one, and only one, concrete image; that of the fireflies. The concept of remembered pleasure is an abstract image, and "staying up late" is an action. Let's see how to rewrite this example to fit the guidelines.

EXAMPLE:
pleasure remembered
staying up late
catching fireflies

Now it is a matter of changing the action of "staying up late" into a concrete image by changing the second line to read "late evening" or "past bedtime". It takes a little more thought to change the abstract idea of "pleasure remembered" into a concrete image. To do this, come up with something concrete that would indicate that the writer is remembering something pleasant. One thing I think we can all relate to would be smiles.

There is nothing wrong with having actions in your haiku, however the example we are using already has one action, that of catching fireflies.

Rule 15: Keep it real and immediate

If you are remembering something, it is not happening right now. It is not real either – it is a memory. In haiku the subject matter should be both real and immediate. There is nothing wrong with writing about a real moment that you remember clearly, but you want to convey it as though it is happening right now. So what changes will turn this abstract thinking into a concrete image and make the image real and immediate at the same time? Try a few changes of your own and then see what you think of this.

Children's smiles
up past bedtime
chasing fireflies

These changes have taken care of the last two guidelines, but notice how we have created a run-on sentence with choppy rhythm. We can smooth this out by either making lines one and three shorter, or by making line two longer. The first method might leave us something like this:

smiles
after bedtime
fireflies

The second method could end up something like this:

laughing children
on the lawn after bedtime
chasing fireflies

Ask yourself – does it make you feel like you are there? If you were the reader, would you feel what the poet felt? Which do you prefer – and why?

Section IV – Viewpoint

- Avoid judgments
- Avoid negativity
- Avoid being too sweet
- Don't humanize non-human elements
- Understand clichés, metaphors and similes

In this category we have grouped together some guidelines which, taken together, set the tone of your haiku. Now that you are comfortable with the more rudimentary guidelines, you are ready to take your haiku to the next level.

At this level you will learn to become more of an observer – simply an observer; not a judge. Nothing in nature is inherently good or bad – it is only humans who judge things to be one or the other. If we avoid making any judgments, our haiku will be neither negative nor sticky-sweet. It should be fairly obvious that any preaching or philosophizing would be judgmental as well, but a guideline about showing emotion might not be quite so easy to relate to being judgmental. When we put our own emotions and feelings into words we are also making a judgment of a sort – we are telling the reader what they "should" feel in this situation.

You will soon notice something else about haiku that follows this group of guidelines – they have more meaning. When we make a judgment or put a label on something we are writing about, we limit the layers of meaning it can have. By simply observing nature and reporting what we see, the haiku we write can have several different layers of meaning, depending on who is reading it and what kind of experiences they are going through at the time they read it.

Rule 16: Avoid judgments

When you make judgments or use judgmental words, what you are actually doing is telling the readers what they "should" think or feel.

EXAMPLE:

threatening clouds

This line should simply describe the clouds and let the reader decide how that makes them feel.

large, black clouds or towering clouds

Can you feel a difference? It is similar to the difference between hearing a program over the radio and watching it on television. When the listener has the opportunity to create their own mind-picture of the "beautiful woman" or the "scary house" they are free to choose exactly the images that stir up those emotions or feelings within themselves. When you present the viewer with a ready-made embodiment of what is beautiful or scary, you always run the risk that they will not agree with your depiction which will prevent them from getting into the story fully. See if you can feel the difference between these two haiku;

no one to play with
beautiful golden setter
waits with loving eyes

Here the writer has not only told the story, but also told the reader how to feel and what to think. Line three goes as far as to tell us what the dog is thinking! The reader of course is free to agree or disagree, but you have left the reader nothing to ponder and expand upon. This is what makes haiku like the example above the type of poem that you read once and put aside. Notice how the haiku example below does the opposite.

prom dress
sweet pink fall of ruffles
never worn

In this haiku the reader is simply reporting what is observed, and making no judgments. The reader is then left to ponder what is happening here. Does this dress belong to a girl who didn't get asked to the prom? Perhaps she had a date for the prom and something happened between the time she bought her dress and the night of the dance...what might that have been? Perhaps the dress belongs to no one; it might be on display in a shop window an object of dreams for little girls too young to go to the prom, or a middle-aged woman remembering her youth. Perhaps it is being viewed by an awestruck young girl who can't believe her good fortune at going to the prom in the first dress she ever had that was not a hand-me-down. Do you see how saying less makes the story bigger? When you add your own judgments to your observations, you cut the story short and do not engage the reader.

Rule 17: Do not try to convey a message

Your haiku is not the place to convey a message, lesson or philosophy of any kind. We have plenty of writing forms designed to teach a lesson or share a philosophy of life, but haiku is not one of them. Anytime the writer delivers a message or lesson, that writer is making the judgment that one choice is right and another choice is wrong. This guideline is a refinement of the guideline against judgments. How does the example below make you feel – calm and tranquil, or at least mildly stirred up?

EXAMPLE:

a war-torn childhood
hard to play among landmines
bombs hurt everyone

Here we have both unacceptable subject matter and a writer who is trying to preach to the reader about the horrors of war. There is nothing wrong with the poet's opinion; however, haiku is not the place to express it. There is also a strong over-lap of imposing your philosophy on the reader and telling the reader what to feel. One purpose of haiku is giving your reader something to think about, and when you tell them what to think you take away that opportunity.

Rule 18: Avoid negativity

In haiku, the object is to transmit a calm and soothing tone. To do this we need to avoid all evidence of negativity – even something as subtle as using the word 'no'. If you were writing your haiku about a sky that had no clouds, it is more positive to describe it as "a cloudless sky" or "a clear blue sky" rather than "a sky with no clouds". Read through some more examples so you can get a feeling for the difference it makes.

empty plates instead of *no food*
seven shiny pieces instead of *broken mirror*
goes fast instead of *doesn't last*
free time instead of *no plans*

Read the following examples to see how avoiding negativity can make your haiku stronger. In this example the writer is relating what he saw while walking on the beach at low tide.

EXAMPLE A:
a walk on the beach
no waves to greet me today
the tide is out

This might almost sound whiny to some people as the writer is subtly complaining about the fact that there are no waves and the tide is out. If the writer instead were to concentrate on what was there, we might read something like this:

EXAMPLE B:

a walk at low tide
view the sea's hidden treasures
outdoor museum

The negative attitude of the writer of example A is reflected in the words used and most likely reflected in the reality of his world as well. When we are focused on what we *don't* have it is easy to miss what is right in front of us.

Once you get in the habit of thinking this way as you compose haiku, you will begin to do the same thing in the other parts of your life.

Instead of concentrating on what is missing, you will begin to focus on what has taken its place. It's a very subtle difference, but once you form the habit of writing your haiku this way, you will begin to think this way on an everyday basis as well. When you go to the cafeteria at lunch, instead of thinking "they have no lasagna today" you will think instead, "they have spaghetti today". Or rather than thinking "I have no job" when your department gets downsized, you will think "Now I have time to finish my book."

This is the kind of thinking that can open up possibilities for you, instead of closing doors. You will stop thinking about all the reasons you *can't* do something and start noticing what you *can* do. Remember that whatever we focus on is what we are going to attract more of into our lives. So when you practice removing negativity from your haiku, this habit will extend to the rest of your life and you will begin to experience less negativity around you.

Rule 19: Avoid being too sweet

You don't want to be negative, but you must however, be careful not to swing too far in the other direction. You may think it is very uplifting and inspiring to write about how glorious things are, or how wonderful they make you feel. However when you are doing this, you set up a negative judgment for the opposite conditions. When you say "sunny days are good" or "beautiful summer day" you are suggesting that cloudy days are bad. And when you say that spring makes you feel hopeful, you are implying that the reader will find winter depressing.

Read through the example below to see how a little editing can tell the same story about spring approaching without labeling spring "desirable" and winter "undesirable."

EXAMPLE:

flower buds bursting
stream free of icy prison
lovely things to come

This story could be expressed this way:

a stream moves freely
distant garden filled with buds
faint smells of the thaw

These changes allow the reader to decide for themselves what feelings this scene brings out. Some readers may very well feel hope or enthusiasm, while for others these feelings might be tinged with a small taste of sadness for passing of a peaceful, slower-moving winter season that offers the opportunity to turn inward.
This, like the guideline about avoiding negativity, is basically just a refinement on the most important guideline about avoiding judgments.
When you construct your narrative, you have the option of choosing what words will convey what you experienced. When you choose the right words, there is no need to spell anything out for the reader. For example, if you are writing a haiku about the coming of winter, you have the choice of saying:

winter looms
or
winter beckons

Read each line out loud and pause before reading the next line. Can you feel the difference in your thoughts when the writer uses a different verb to express the concept of winter coming? How might you complete a haiku using the first line shown? How might you complete a haiku that begins with the last example? Would that tell the same story? Try completing a haiku with an opening line of "winter approaches." You will probably find that you have a lot more options.

You can do the same thing with adverbs and adjectives as well. Think about a street – now think about how it makes you feel and find a word to convey that to the reader without specifying your emotion openly.
Is it a:

trendy street
or
a deserted street
or
a dead-end street
or
a tree-lined street

If you were to add a second or third line to make a haiku from these beginnings, see how different they might be.
    EXAMPLE A

trendy street
shop windows bursting
anticipation

    EXAMPLE B

deserted street
noises from nowhere
suddenly sirens

What feelings do you get from the first haiku…from the second? What time of day came into your mind? Were you alone, or were there other people? How much money would you like to be carrying on the trendy street…on the deserted street? What do you think happened next? Now try reversing the opening lines of the two examples notice that you have two entirely different stories.

    EXAMPLE A (2)

deserted street
shop windows bursting
anticipation

    EXAMPLE B (2)

trendy street
noises from nowhere
suddenly sirens

Would you answer the questions the same way when the first lines are reversed? On which street were the shop windows bursting with enticing merchandise and on which street were the windows bursting because of something thrown through the glass? What did you anticipate when you were walking down the "deserted street"? And what did you anticipate walking down the trendy street?

On which street were the sirens responding to a shoplifter? On which street were the sirens responding to looters? On which street where the sirens responding to a heart attack victim? On which street where the sirens responding to a stabbing victim?

It's pretty easy to pick out the "right" answers, isn't it? And in these examples we only changed the first word from "trendy" to "deserted." Are you beginning to getting a sense of how powerful words can be? When you choose just the right one, you are making a tremendous change in how your reader or listener perceives what else you have to say. In this way, the discipline of writing haiku will make you a more eloquent and persuasive speaker as well as a better poet.

Rule 20: Do not Humanize Non-human Elements

In haiku we are observing nature and reporting what we see. We must be careful not to assign human actions and emotions to natural objects, or even to animals. At one time or another – either in prose or poetry – I'm sure everyone has read a line like the following:

The birds were singing happily

How do we know they were happy? They may have been communicating with one another about an approaching storm, or wondering where their next meal was coming from. So try to keep your haiku free of mischievous frogs, lonely crescent moons or flowers that talk to you.

There is a subtle difference between the wording in the previous examples and the use of similar "human activity" type words when we are describing the way something moves for example. When we say something like "sunlight dancing on the water" we do not literally mean that the sunlight is doing the tango – here we are conveying a light, sporadic, movement that tells the reader that the water is moving quickly and rhythmically and thus changing the points where the sunlight is reflected. Read the two examples below and see if you can tell the difference.

EXAMPLE A:

rising sun beckons
flowers waiting off-stage
to welcome spring

EXAMPLE B:

snowfall in darkness
in dawn's light the pine trees
bow under the weight

This guideline can be very subtle sometimes. A good rule of thumb might be; "if it's not obvious, it's probably okay."

Rule 21: Clichés, Metaphors and Similes

One of the goals of haiku is to make the reader think, but when your reader encounters a timeworn cliché, their mind automatically shuts down. The subconscious mind reaches into a filing cabinet and pulls out the response to the words you have just written. And because the human response to these clichés follows such an ingrained formula, you may also be guilty of telling the reader what to feel. How many times have you read about an emotional rollercoaster, or a beehive of activity? Sometimes a cliché can be a topic instead of a word or a phrase. I think we've all been presented with the following topics more than once and in pictures as well as words.

The brave weed pushing through the crack in the sidewalk
Kids ignoring the toy and playing with the box it came in
Early spring flowers dusted with snow

If the haiku begins with one of these, is there any reason to read beyond the first line? We have become so accustomed to filmmakers, advertisers and magazine editors spoon-feeding us information that we are becoming deprived of any opportunities to use our imagination. The information supplied to us by the media is designed in a way that attempts to ensure that we all get exactly the same information. Haiku is intended to give the readers food for thought, not to digest it for them. With only 17 syllables to tell your story; do you really want to share the stage with someone else's work? It is far better to reach for ordinary words that are heavy with connotation.

Similes and metaphors certainly have a place in haiku as long as you recognize when one has become a cliché. A simile is a figure of speech that compares two things that are alike in some way usually separating them by the words 'like' or 'as'. Examples would be; "busy as a bee" or "like a bat out of hell."

A metaphor is figure of speech that describes two things that are very different, but alike in one way, as though one actually *was* the other. Sometimes you might say that a difficult task you finished was "a breeze," or if you had trouble with it, you may have said "it was a bear." Nobody would think the task was actually a weather phenomenon or an animal, but they would know the first response meant it was easy and the latter meant that it was hard.

In our everyday conversations similes and metaphors are a kind of short-hand we use to convey something quickly and easily but when over-used, they can be clichés. In haiku, using similes and metaphors in new and unexpected way can be a very powerful and poetic way to enrich your narrative. Just make sure it is fresh.

Keeping a journal of your work is a great way to see how much progress you have made. You may like to arrange your haiku chronologically or you may prefer to keep them together by topic. Some people like to have just one haiku on each page leaving space for revisions and refinements as they begin to develop their own style. A loose leaf binder works well, so that you can add pages as you wish and rearrange your work as you cover more topics.

Section V–Grammatical Conventions

I've put it off for as long as possible, but since are we practicing the writing craft, there is no getting around the subject of grammar. The good news is that the grammatical conventions we are working with here are almost as short and to the point as haiku itself.

- Stay in the present tense
- Limits for nouns and verbs
- End with a noun
- Use singular forms
- Avoid personal pronouns

Rule 22: Stay in the present tense

Write your haiku in the present tense (trees blossom), not past tense (trees have blossomed) or future tense (trees will blossom). As you become accustomed to following this guideline in your writing, your mind will develop new habits and you will begin to notice that this way of thinking carries over into the rest of your life as well.

As it becomes more natural for you to concentrate on what is happening now instead of ruminating about the past or agonizing about the future, you will be happy to notice that you are experiencing less guilt, worry and regret. This is what eastern philosophers call "being in the moment." The wonderful part about living in the present is that it is the only moment we have any control over.

There are actually two parts to this guideline; one is to stay in the here and now by using the present tense, and the other has to do with focusing so closely on a single moment that time seems to stand still. Any time that you switch tenses within your 17 syllable limit, you are going to be scattering focus so widely that the reader will have difficulty absorbing the narrative.

EXAMPLE:
Winter is coming
Squirrels have hidden their nuts
Enjoy summer now!

The first line refers to the future, the second line refers to the past, and yet the third line exhorts the reader to live in the present! Read the haiku for yourself and see how difficult it is to form a clear picture. As you read these three short lines, can you feel your mind being pulled away as each new line begins? Just as your mind begins to form one picture, you are asked to think about something else. It's enough to give you motion sickness! Read on to see how a little re-writing changes the whole picture.

EDITED EXAMPLE:
autumn advances
acorns hidden far and wide
secret preparations

This version lets us imagine what is coming while keeping us in the present. It would be redundant to write a haiku about staying in the present because any haiku that you write according to the guidelines we are using here is already conveying that idea by doing exactly that – staying in the present moment.

Much of the tranquility that we feel when reading haiku is a result of staying in the present: The present is a very peaceful, non-judgmental place to be. No matter what is going on in your life, if you can forget about the past and trust in the future, you will discover that right this moment, everything is okay.

Try it for yourself – think about a really low point in your life when you felt certain your world was going to collapse around you. Now condense this into a story of no more than one paragraph. For example – a customer service representative who applied for a supervisory opening lost out to another candidate. In the heat of the moment, the story might like sound something like this:

Step 1: Tell your story

I work harder than anybody in my department. I am the one who handles the most difficult customers. I gave up most of my social life and lost a lot of sleep worrying about what I could do to make myself the best employee this department ever had.

I applied for a promotion when an opening came up and they gave it someone else. Someone who doesn't have half as much experience as I do and won't be as willing to put out the effort required to learn all the ins and outs of running a customer service center.

Now I will have to train the person who beat me out for the job while answering everybody else's questions and still doing my own job but I'm not the one who is getting the title and the raise. I'm going to be stuck forever where I am not appreciated, because the job market here is so tight, I'll never find anything else.

Step 2: Retell your story while staying in the present
First, remove all thoughts and perceptions about the past.

A departmental promotion was given to someone who has less experience and probably won't be as willing to put out the effort required to learn all the ins and outs of running a customer service center. Now I will have to train the person who beat me out for the job while answering everybody else's questions and still doing my own job but I'm not the one who is getting the title and the raise. I'm going to be stuck forever here where I am not appreciated, because the job market here is so tight, I'll never find anything else.

Now eliminate the lines that refer to the future. What does that leave us for a story that is completely in the present? Just – *Somebody else got the promotion I applied for.*

This is all that is actually happening at the moment, so the story is simply:

Someone was promoted to customer service supervisor.

Can you see how this could be a happy story if that someone were the writer's spouse, child or good friend?

More importantly, you see what a difference it would make if the writer had not applied for this opening? If not for the past (wanting and going after this job), there would be no negative feelings attached to this story.

So when we remove the regrets and bitterness about the past and the writer's worries about the future, nothing bad is happening. In the present moment, everything is okay. Our haiku might read something like this:

Step 3:
changes afoot
coworker today
supervisor tomorrow

Can you almost feel the writer smiling as this story is written as haiku?

Rule 23: Limits for nouns and verbs

One of the basics of haiku is the idea of using nouns instead of verbs. Writing without verbs tends to celebrate being rather than doing and this shift in focus will help slow you down in a hectic world. For our purposes, "doing" is defined as any focused, goal-oriented activity. This would include things like making the bed, playing football, reading or dancing as well talking on the telephone or watching television. On other side of this coin is "being". This is our authentic state where we are merely experiencing the current moment with no thoughts of the future or the past. Usually when we are doing something, the focus will be on the future (cramming for finals that will lead to a degree, or revising our budget to increase retirement savings) or the past, (filing an amended tax return, or cleaning up the chili that splattered in the microwave last night).

When you are in a state of being, you do not have to expend any energy in the present moment to achieve that state. If you have a medical degree, you are a doctor. That is to say simply by existing you are "being" a doctor. When you are seeing a patient or performing surgery, you are "doing" those things that a doctor does, but even when you are sleeping or playing golf, you are still "being" a doctor. We can often determine someone's state of being by what they are doing, but be careful not to confuse the two – just because someone is giving you medical advice does not mean they are a doctor.

With haiku we try to achieve a peaceful state of serenity by focusing on what just "is" rather than what is happening to us. This also makes it easier to drop our judgments and feel at one with the scene that is being described. Instead of focusing on the activity that created this scene or what might be the result of what is happening right now, we also make it easier for the reader to stay in the present. Minimizing the number of verbs in our haiku is the most powerful way of shifting the reader's focus to being, rather than doing. Let's look at some examples and see how this works.

Water rises
Rain falls on the meadow
And fills the river

It not only becomes exhausting to try to follow the water as it rises and falls and then fills; it paints three separate pictures in this tiny narrative. In haiku, that is two pictures too many. You need to stay in the moment and paint one vivid picture if you are going to transmit the calm mood that haiku is aiming for. You can take any of the three ideas in our example and write a haiku around each separate action indicated by the verbs in the first example.

Working with the idea of rising water, we may get something like this:

*water rises
past yesterday's exposed roots
on to new levels*

To focus the readers' attention on falling rain you might go this route:

*generous skies
rain on the grasslands
leaves sodden acres*

As for the river being filled up, your haiku might look like this example:

*afternoon deluge
meadowland runoff
fills the river*

Read the four examples and see how much more difficult it is to form a clear mind picture where the writer tries to combine a series of actions. Read the three revised versions one at a time and notice how much difference there is in the images they bring to mind. Can you feel why all three should not be in one haiku? Anytime you use more than two verbs in one haiku, you run the risk of scattering the reader's focus and disrupting the calm and tranquil mood you are trying to create.

Most haiku masters will use a maximum of three nouns and one verb. Using too many nouns in one haiku creates many of the same problems we encounter when using too many verbs. The number of nouns you can use without disturbing your reader's focus is just a little bit higher. The reason for this is that when properly used, a noun can actually *increase* the focus rather than lessening it. Read the two examples below to see what this means in practice.

EXAMPLE A:
tawny tweed carpet
soft pine needle patterns on
yesterday's leaves

EXAMPLE B:
a bruised sky hangs low
summer reigns majestically
while trees bow to nothing

In example A, the writer has actually used five nouns – tweed, carpet, pine needle, patterns and leaves. In example B we have just three nouns – sky, summer and trees.
Which example is more cohesive? Can you feel why? Two of the nouns in the first example (tweed and patterns) are descriptive nouns that are being used as adjectives in this haiku. If we eliminate those words from our count, the poems have an equal number of nouns, and both haiku relate a story quite well

The primary reason for this is that they are all details of the same image – pine needles have fallen on leaves making a pattern on the ground. The mind's eye focuses on one image which is made more vivid by the inclusion of these details. The clever use of the words "tawny" and "yesterday's" let us know that these are autumn leaves that have fallen from the tree – and without using the words fall or autumn. The words "tweed" and "patterns" are working together to direct the reader's attention to a clear picture of what the writer is seeing at this moment. If you experiment with eliminating any of the words in this haiku, the picture is less clear and not nearly as vivid. Anytime your haiku becomes stronger by eliminating one or more of the words, then you know that these are unnecessary; and we find no unnecessary words in this haiku.

In example B, the three nouns are sky, summer and trees. By now you should realize that the word "summer" is a haiku "no-no" – if the writer constructs the picture vividly enough, the reader will know what season it is without being told. Now, think about what happens when you try get a picture from these two nouns – your mind's eye has no choice but to dart first up to the sky and then down to the trees. It is possible to use both nouns without creating this effect. One way would be to say something about "trees meeting the sky", but the writer didn't do this in our example and the result is not very calming. The bottom line is; it is not simply the *number* of nouns that you use, but how you use them.

How could the writer improve this haiku by reducing the number of nouns? Let's begin our editing by eliminating the word summer, since it violates another guideline as well. Since this haiku is talking about thunderclouds, the reader can easily determine the season without the word "summer". This leaves us with "trees" and "skies" and our task will be finding a way to bring them closer together visually so that the reader can stay focused. Try this on your own and then read the possibility below.

EDITED EXAMPLE B:
Heavy-limbed maples
bend under ominous skies
low and converging

This opening line immediately sets the season as the reader will know that tree leaves are fullest at the height of summer. The single verb – bend – in the second line paints a picture of a wind strong enough to bend the trees. The word "ominous" will make the reader feel that that the sky is probably quite dark and most likely filled with large clouds. With the combined message of dark clouds, strong winds and trees in full leaf, the reader has been painted a clear picture of a summer thunderstorm. By using three nouns or less, a writer is required to choose exactly the right words – whether nouns, verbs, adjectives or adverbs – to tell the story in a maximum of 17 syllables. When you have been practicing haiku long enough that this becomes second nature to you, you are going to be a much better speaker because you will be more adept at choosing exactly the right words.

Rule 24: End with a noun

This is one of those guidelines that many people ignore either because they think haiku has too many guidelines already [and believe me, there are many more conventions in writing haiku than we are covering here] or because they fail to see how it makes their haiku stronger. I have chosen to include this in our selection of guidelines because it is one that instills discipline and promotes the serenity that we are trying to achieve by writing haiku.
Ending with a noun brings closure. When our narrative ends in a verb, it is almost like some unfinished business hanging over us, and unfinished business promotes stress, not serenity. Using the example below, can you see why the reader may be left waiting for the other shoe to drop; wondering where these clouds are sailing to or what they are sailing towards? In most cases, the existing haiku needs only to be rearranged in order to avoid ending with a verb, but in some cases only a complete re-write can give you the effect you desire. Read and compare the following two examples and see which you feel is stronger.

EXAMPLE A:

against sapphire skies
a gilt frame of sycamores
cobweb clouds sailing

EXAMPLE B:

cobweb clouds sailing
in a gilt frame of sycamores
against sapphire skies

Don't worry if you do not agree – remember, we make no judgments in haiku! If your haiku does not lend itself easily to ending with a noun, you should at least avoid ending with a verb. You want to invite the mind of the reader to explore deeper layers of your narrative as given – not search for probable endings to the story. It can be a very subtle difference sometimes, but follow the two examples below and see if you can feel it.

EXAMPLE C:

windows fully open
behind billowing curtains
hear the caged bird sing

In example C the haiku ends with a verb that tells us the caged bird is singing. Does the caged bird sing of freedom lost? Or is it singing with happiness at having the protection and security of the cage knowing there are predators outside? Maybe it is grateful that it knows where its next meal is coming from and does not have to forage like the wild birds on the other side of the window. Let's do some rearranging and write the same haiku in such a way that it ends with a noun.

EXAMPLE D:

cage full of bird-song
untied curtains billow out
wide open windows

In example D, the singing bird takes center stage from the opening line and the phrasing that follows provides the contrast of the cage with the freedom of open windows. The poem written this way still leaves the reader plenty to ponder about, but the boundaries have been set for this narrative. Having the action of a verb at the end of the last line gives the feeling that something more is going to happen, making the story feel unfinished even though it is giving the same amount of information.

Rule 25: Use singular forms

This is not a hard and fast guideline for every haiku you write, but in general using the singular form instead of the plural will bring you closer to what we are trying achieve. The goal I refer to is that of focusing, and when you write in the singular, it will naturally concentrate your focus. Focusing on a single object or event also will help you to see the details that are required to paint a vivid picture in such a tiny narrative. Read the two examples below and see if you agree.

EXAMPLE A:

tulips and daffodils
long gone but not forgotten
spring's welcome return

EXAMPLE B:

the first tulip opens
bold scarlet shape confirming
the rumor of spring

After all, how many tulips does it take for us to believe spring is here? And do we need to see *both* tulips and daffodils? Either one of these words can be used as a seasonal word to indicate early spring, but using both of them is virtually the same as repeating a word. Remember our rule of thumb – if your haiku can tell the story without the word, it should be eliminated. As you read the two examples, which one gives to mind a clearer picture?

Rule 26: Avoid personal pronouns

Using a personal pronoun (like "I", "me" or "our") puts the focus on the writer and creates a limited narrative for the reader. When you take yourself out of the story, you allow the reader to step in. By doing this you allow for multiple interpretations and one of these will speak directly to the reader.

EXAMPLE A:

the rough thawed soil
a velvet-leaved violet
my hesitant foot

EXAMPLE B:

the rough thawed soil
a velvet-leaved violet
hesitant footsteps

As you read example A, it is only natural to try to picture the individual behind the "my" and that creates a distraction. It has also introduced a human element into the haiku since a rabbit would not be writing poetry. Experiment for a while to see how many different mind-pictures you can get from each example and you will come to understand the guideline about avoiding personal pronouns.

Putting it into Practice

The following practical exercises are opportunities, not obligations. Obligations are burdens and opportunities are invitations. These exercises are something that you can do every day to uncover your inner peace and serenity. I invite you to complete as many or few of these as you wish.

There are 28 days of exercises in this book, roughly the time it takes to create a new habit. If you are willing to do one of these each day, you will find yourself developing a new way of forming thoughts. This new way of thinking will bring you to a place of peace and tranquility by helping you to feel acceptance for the perfection in everything; no matter how imperfect it may appear.

If you quiet down daily in formal practice, you will be better able to access this sense of peace in daily interactions because when you are less judgmental you can accept yourself more fully.

If you would like to:

- Balance your mind
- Improve your focus
- Experience less stress
- Have fewer disturbing thoughts
- Feel more peace and self-worth

Make writing haiku one of your daily habits. If you already keep a diary or journal, it is simply a matter of including a narration of your day in the form of a haiku. It could be describing the high point of your day, or a low point or simply a summary of how you feel.

If you have not already created a journal for yourself, this would be a good time to do so. Later on, you will find that reading through your journal is a sure-fire way to overcome any writer's block you might encounter when beginning a new exercise.

Practical Exercises

EXERCISE 1 - SHORT AND SWEET

For the first exercises we are going to begin very simply and our goal will be to write a haiku that follows three of the first five basic guidelines about length and form. These are:

- Maximum of 17 syllables
- Arrange on three lines
- Write without a title

For your topic I would like you to write about something in nature that you traditionally associate with the coming of spring. This might be the first violet or crocus for somebody who lives in the country, or the first day you open the windows on the bus ride home for an urban dweller. It does not matter if you choose Easter bonnets, the first batch of kittens or a slushy sidewalk – simply pick a sign of spring and describe it briefly. If you find it helpful, you can then condense your brief description into a single sentence.

Next, choose the key words that put across your story and arrange them on three lines using no more than 17 syllables.

Compare what you have written to the three basic guidelines above and begin making any changes necessary. Do not be concerned if making one change requires you to make another, during the editing process your concentrated focus will actually begin de-stressing you as you set everything else aside and concentrate on the essence of your narrative.

If you like, you can now transfer your finished haiku to a journal like the one we talked about earlier. Some people like to put just one haiku on each page with space below to accommodate further revisions.

EXERCISE 2 - CREATING THE FLOW

For our second exercise we are going to build on what we have practiced so far and add in the final two of the five basic guidelines which would be:

- Avoid phrases that read like a sentence
- Avoid stops after each line

The topic this time will be winter – you can talk about snow forts, frozen ponds, hot chocolate or Christmas – or any other subject that means winter to you. Create a haiku on this topic just as you did for the last exercise, but this time pay special attention to the flow of what you have written.

If all of the words could be strung into a single sentence, try rearranging them to read more like a short fragment followed by a short phrase. You can also reverse this order so that the first two lines can be read together and the third line stands alone.

If you have either avoided or eliminated the run-on sentence, check the flow to see if it sounds choppy. Would the reader tend to come to a stop at the end of each line? If the haiku reads like a list of three statements or phrases, re-write your haiku so that either the last two or the first two lines flow smoothly together.

How easy was this for you? If you did have problems with flow, was the tendency towards choppiness; or a run-on sentence? As we create more haiku in the following practices, you will undoubtedly have less problems with this, just be careful not to swing from one extreme to the other. You can always refer to the earlier examples of this in Section I to guide you.

If you are keeping a journal, transfer your finished haiku to it now.

EXERCISE 3 - SIMPLIFY

In the next exercise we are going to work on all of the guidelines from Section II. These are some of the easiest rules to abide by and yet these are also the very guidelines that separate haiku from other forms of poetry. To review, these rules are as follows.

- Avoid lines that rhyme
- Use capital letters only on proper nouns
- Use little or no punctuation
- Use commonplace words
- Avoid repeated or unnecessary words

This time the topic will be summer – whatever exemplifies this season to you. Perhaps that would be lemonade stands, or school vacation or even bee stings. Choose a sign of summer that appeals to you and compose a haiku about it. You can continue to write a description first and then condense it if that feels comfortable for you.

Compare what you have written to the list of guidelines above and check to see if you want to make changes. Do any of the lines rhyme? If so, replace one of the rhyming words with another (non-rhyming) word that coveys the same meaning. Sometimes you may have to rearrange the order of your words to make this work. Your haiku should have little or no punctuation, and only proper nouns should be capitalized. If you did put punctuation in your haiku, try removing it. You will probably find that your poem still works, and it probably flows more smoothly.

Would the average reader easily understand the words you have chosen? If not, replace the word in question with one that means the same thing but would be used in everyday communication. Last but not least, read your poem again and see if you have repeated any words. If you have, or if you have used two words with the same meaning, you will want to work on tightening up your narrative to avoid that repetition. I repeat, 17 syllables is our upper limit, but less is okay. Never pad your story to make it fill out the full 17 syllables.

Remember, you are doing this for your own benefit – not mine. So you have the option of skipping any guideline or exercise that you don't think is helpful.

EXERCISE 4 - PUTTING IT ALL TOGETHER

This time we will write a haiku about the last of our seasons – autumn. Again, choose anything that means autumn to you – colorful leaves, bonfires, shortened days or even Halloween. Follow the entire process of choosing a topic, then condensing and arranging it according to the first two sets of guidelines: [Maximum of 17 syllables/Arrange on three lines/Write without a title/Avoid phrasing that reads like a sentence/Avoid stops after each line/Avoid rhyming/Use capital letters only on proper nouns/Use little or no punctuation/Use commonplace words/Avoid repeated or unnecessary words].

By now these should be second nature to you. When ready, transfer your finished work to your journal.

EXERCISE 5 - STRETCH YOURSELF

For this exercise, take the sample poem that follows and rewrite it so that it follows all of the guidelines we have been working with so far. You do not need to use the same words that the writer used; the goal is to tell the same story in accepted haiku form.

Campfire companions;

Underneath a glowing moon,

Bullfrogs out of tune.

Did this poem seem more like haiku after you removed the unnecessary punctuation and capitalization? How did you deal with the rhyming words? You can either choose new words, or simply rearrange the words that you have now.

For example:

campfire companions

glowing moon overhead

bullfrogs out of tune

or

campfire companions

underneath a glowing moon

out of tune bullfrogs

The possibilities are limited only by your imagination.

EXERCISE 6 - TALK YOURSELF CALM

The object of haiku is to create a quiet, tranquil mood. Which of the following examples is stronger haiku according to our guidelines?

afternoon lullabies

all have settled into naps

something to sing about

or

unexpected detour

appointment time approaching

curls melt in the heat

Now, write a haiku of your own about a tranquil moment you have found in your life. It can be very effective to contrast the peace and quiet with noise or bustle, but make sure the focus is on the tranquility.

> *As you transfer your finished work to your journal, remember that you can return to this haiku when you need to capture a feeling of serenity. This is why it is so important to paint such a vivid picture that reading the lines will transport you – or your reader – to the place and time you are writing about.*

EXERCISE 7 - ALONE WITH NATURE

Many of us have had the experience of arriving at the seashore or campground fully expecting peace and relaxation only to discover our destination so crowded with tourists that it is less relaxing than the place we left behind. When we create a mind picture of tranquility on a mountaintop or beside a stream, it usually does not include other humans. Think of the different moods that an artist can create by painting a landscape that has people in it versus one with no human intervention. This difference in mood applies to haiku as well. To create a truly calming mood, haiku focuses on nature with a minimum of human intervention – none is better.

For today's Exercise bring to mind a place that is normally full of human activity, but write your haiku about what it would be like to experience this place when no people are around. This might be a beach in the winter or a café before it opens or perhaps the school playground at night. Use your imagination and focus on one small aspect of this familiar place that can look so unfamiliar without the usual human activity.

> *As you transfer your finished work to your journal, make a check of the basic rules of haiku we have been working with so far to see if you have developed a habit of writing this way automatically.*

EXERCISE 8 - IN SYNCH WITH THE SEASONS

One of the most effective ways to achieve tranquility in your life is to stay in synch with the seasons. With modern technology like indoor lighting and central heating, it is easy to get out of touch with not only what season it is, but even what time of day. Have you ever been in a casino and completely lost track of the time because of the lack of clocks and windows?

Or have you ever been totally absorbed in a movie and discovered when you exited the theater that that while you were watching, a storm has sprung up and turned the sunny day into a wet one? That disconcerting feeling you get when you go outside and discover day has turned to night or sun has turned into rain can be a subtle source of stress. If you were more in touch with nature – either outside or near a window – you would have seen gradual signs of the change coming, like the sun sinking lower or clouds moving in.

For today's exercise, see how well synchronized you are with the current season by writing a haiku about the season you are in right now. Notice what is unique about today as opposed to last month – are the days shorter? Are there more or fewer leaves on the trees? What shade of blue is the sky – and how is this different from the sky colors in another season? Test your powers of observation while incorporating the basic guidelines of haiku.

As you transfer your finished work to your journal, you may want to begin sorting your haiku into categories by season.

EXERCISE 9 - USING SEASONAL WORDS/SPRING

Although we work closely with nature and the seasons in haiku, it is a hallmark of strong haiku not to designate the season by name. When you paint a clear picture of nature, the reader will know what the season it without you naming it. In section III you will find several examples of what seasonal words are and in this next series of exercises you will be working with these so that they will become second nature to you.

For this exercise, write a haiku about a pond or lake you have seen, without naming the season. For a haiku about spring you might describe apple trees blossoming on the shore, or newly-hatched ducklings learning how to swim. If you are picturing a summer scene, you might describe a swarm of gnats, or the drone of bumble bees in the distance. Can you see how these details immediately bring to mind a certain season? Feel the difference between golden leaves floating in pond as opposed to a dry brown leaf blowing across its icy surface.

Let's begin with springtime as we start this series of four exercises.

EXERCISE 10 - USING SEASONAL WORDS/SUMMER

There were probably several different ideas that came to you when describing spring. Have you ever realized how numbers can make the reader's mind turn to a particular season? In the summer and fall there is a natural tendency to think in terms of large numbers because these are the seasons of abundance. In the summertime there will be a profusion of flowers, while a single bloom will make us realize it is springtime. In winter, a single withered leaf might be left hanging on the tree, while in autumn the hills are covered with masses of brilliantly colored leaves.

This time we will use summertime as the topic of our exercise and see if you can find a way to work the concepts of numbers or quantities into your narrative.

If you have done other work on the topic of summertime, put them together in your journal of finished work.

EXERCISE 11 - USING SEASONAL WORDS/FALL

Now that we have worked with numbers/quantities, let's turn our attention to colors. When you write in terms of black, white or shades of grey, most people will think about winter, while a palette ranging from gold to burgundy makes almost everybody think of autumn. When describing deep or vibrant shades of green, you will draw your readers' mind towards the foliage and grasses of summer while pale shades of yellow-green most often bring to mind the young growth of early spring.

Autumn will be the topic of this exercise and this time see if you can find a way to introduce some form of color as your seasonal word.

When you were choosing a seasonal reference, which came more for naturally for you, using numbers or using colors?

EXERCISE 12 - USING SEASONAL WORDS/WINTER

Now that we've worked with colors and numbers; what other seasonal indicators can you think of? List some that come to mind for you. Was one of them food? If you stop to think about it, the average person's menu changes quite a bit from season to season. Every season brings certain fruits and vegetables that are cheap and plentiful when they are in season. For this reason a ripe peach will make your reader think of summer and a big pumpkin is likely to make their thoughts turn to fall. Some foods are available only when the season brings the market – like snow cones at the beach, or cotton candy at the fair. Other foods are simply more appealing in one season than another, like a hearty stew in the winter or a crisp salad in the summer.

For our final exercise in this series, we will work with the season of winter. See if you can find a way to work in food as a seasonal indicator. How many of you thought about Christmas cookies? Or hot chocolate? Was the food that came to your mind a family tradition?

As you completed the past four exercises did you have any trouble avoiding the name of the season? How easy would it be for the average reader to know what season you are writing about?

> *For further practice try writing some seasonal haiku using some of the five senses (taste, touch, sight, sound and smell) that you haven't worked with yet.*

EXERCISE 13 - KEEPING IT REAL

Another one of the guidelines we talked about in Section III is using concrete images rather than abstract thoughts. For this next series of exercises, we will choose a feeling or emotion to work with and it will be your task to find concrete images that will evoke that feeling for the reader. Two sample haiku are given below – read them both and decide which one comes closer to describing the way you might feel after suffering a personal loss.

grape vines stripped empty

a last straggling leaf trembles

at the howling wind

Or

upright daffodils

by the dozens on a hill

cold and grayness gone

It is natural for some people to associate melancholy with autumn (after the grapes have been harvested) and hope with springtime (when daffodils appear). In strong haiku the writer would never use a word like "sad" – but words like "stripped", "straggling" and "howling" are words that will convey the empty feeling of loss.

Think about a time in your life when you were eagerly anticipating something that you expected to be wonderful. Perhaps this could be a date for the prom, or a college acceptance letter – or maybe Christmas. When you have the feeling firmly in your mind, write a haiku that coveys this feeling without naming it.

> *Was this exercise easy or hard for you? How much of a role, if any, did one of the seasons play in getting your feeling across to the reader? How about colors or numbers?*

EXERCISE 14 - IMMEDIACY

Another guideline in Section III refers to subject matter that is both real and immediate. By immediate we mean "near" as in very close at hand or deep in our hearts. This is why somebody writing haiku at the seashore should not be writing about the mountains and vice versa. There is nothing wrong with writing about something you remember clearly, but the more immediate your subject matter is, the better you will be able to write about it. Read the following examples and decide which writer was actually looking at the subject matter and which one was writing about the subject of a book read recently.

Japanese schoolgirls

happily sharing mud pies

chopstick twigs

or

limestone fence

top row missing members

half buried in the earth

For this next exercise I want you to bring to mind a nearby scene, from your yard or another part of the house that you cannot see from where you are now. Write a haiku about this following as many of the guidelines as you feel comfortable with at this point.

Now take your notebook to where you can look at the actual scene and see if you notice any details that were not in your "mind picture" of this subject as you were writing about it. If it is a scene from nature, has it changed since the last time you saw it? Either write another haiku, or make changes to the first one you wrote.

Read both of your latest haiku. Does the second one feel fresher and more personal to you? Transfer your finished work to your journal.

EXERCISE 15 – AVOID REPETITION

See how you can revise this sample haiku to eliminate any repeated words.

yellow daffodils
open their golden throats
symphony of spring

Although "yellow" and "golden" are not exactly the same word, they do have the same meaning as it relates to this haiku, and would therefore be considered a repeated word. Using both words does not strengthen the narrative in any way.

> *The guidelines should be second nature to you by now. For the next two weeks write and edit using the instincts you've developed in the guided exercises. You can strengthen your grasp on any of these guidelines by going through the examples in the various exercises and finding and fixing any instances that do not conform.*

EXERCISE 16 – DON'T HUMANIZE NON-HUMAN ELEMENTS

Rework the following sample to create a similar story while removing any human characteristics.

a shy sun playing
peek-a-boo with the morning haze
who will win today

> *Edit to incorporate all of our guidelines and then transfer your finished poem to the appropriate part of your journal.*

EXERCISE 17 – ENDING WITH A NOUN

How would you make this one conform to the guideline?

deep nautical sighs
sand sprinkled with rumors of
what the ocean holds

> *Transfer your finished work to your personal journal.*

EXERCISE 18 – REMOVING PERSONAL PRONOUNS

Use your creativity to retell this story without the use of pronouns.

Storm- bruised skies hang low
sleep accepts my surrender
damp leaves in darkness

> *Transfer your finished work to your personal journal.*

EXERCISE 19 – USING ORDINARY WORDS

Don't make your reader reach for their dictionary; use your thesaurus to rework this haiku and make the story clear for the average reader.

confabulating
silver hair to rheumy eye
history is rewritten

> *Can you hear how the haiku is actually made stronger by using simpler words?*

EXERCISE 20 – NON-RHYMING LINES

Show how this narrative can be rewritten with no rhyming lines.

here's just me and you
beneath a wide sky of blue
with nothing to do

You don't need to use any of the words in our example; just write a haiku that creates the same feeling and season, without any negativity.

EXERCISE 21 – REDUCE SYLLABLE COUNT

Write your own narrative to paint this word-picture using 17 syllables or less.

stars hanging high
against the velvet canvas of
skies the wind swept clean

Either rewrite this example to conform to the guideline or stretch yourself by painting your own word picture of a night sky.

EXERCISE 22 – USING SIMILES AND METAPHORS

Tell this story in your own words without using "like" or "as".

wispy clouds open
like a theater curtain
showcasing the stars

> By now most likely you not only "get it", but you've probably developed your own style. Remember: first learn the rules and then break them.

Now let's take those new skills you've honed and have some fun with them.

EXERCISE 23 – JUST FOR FUN

Think of a favorite story from your childhood; like Cinderella, or The Little Engine that Could; then use the steps outlined in the first section to reduce the story to a haiku.

Transfer your finished work to your personal journal.

EXERCISE 24 – JUST FOR FUN

Select a story from the news and reduce it to a haiku.

Remember, no messages and no judgements – stretch yourself by choosing a story that brings up strong feelings for you. Perhaps the real stretch would be using a news story that leaves you feeling indifferent.

EXERCISE 25 – JUST FOR FUN

Choose a classic like Romeo and Juliet, a Tale of Two Cities, or Catcher in the Rye and reduce the story to a haiku that meets all of the guidelines we are using.

This can be even more fun if you have formed a writing group – either have all members use the same book, or let them choose their own book and have the rest of the group guess what book they are using when the haikus are read aloud at the next meeting.

EXERCISE 26 – JUST FOR FUN

Think of the worst moment you've had this week and make it into a haiku. Do your feelings change when you read what you have written? Were you able to reduce the emotional charge simply by removing any judgements from the narration?

How does today's haiku compare to your earlier work?

EXERCISE 27 – JUST FOR FUN

Repeat Exercise 26 using a feeling of accomplishment from the recent past. How do you feel when you read your finished haiku? If you were to reread this haiku when you were feeling discouraged, would it still give you the same feeling that you had when it happened? If not, what can you change so that it does revive that feeling?

Transfer your finished work to your personal journal.

EXERCISE 28 – JUST FOR FUN

Write a haiku that you can print out and post in a place where you can go to it any time you are feeling stressed, discouraged or indecisive. It could be a happy thought to remind you that life will always bring you good times along with the bad. Or it could be about a time when you felt discouraged, (one not too recent) that allows you to see how the negative feelings you had at that time dissolved as time passed.

All of these exercises can be repeated indefinitely by choosing different subjects for your haiku. You might also enjoy creating your own collections such as haikus on gratitude or haikus on love. You could even include one in your greeting cards for a truly personal touch. You might make a favorite haiku part of the signature on your email, or include a timely haiku in your blog if you have one. There are lots of enjoyable ways to make haiku part of your daily routine; if you are already in the habit of keeping a daily journal or diary you can summarize the day with a haiku or even substitute the haiku itself for an entry when you need de-stress after a bad day.

Never lose sight of the fact that it's not about writing the perfect haiku, but rather about dropping judgements and staying in the present.

Summing it All Up

The power of haiku comes from creating it. The practice of writing one haiku a day for at least 28 days will have you seeing the world differently. By the end of the month, you will have uncovered a well of tranquility inside yourself that you never realized was there.

What we practice grows stronger. We are always practicing and thereby reinforcing some mental or emotional pattern. The mind is continually making judgements, assigning a quality of positivity or negativity – deciding whether to accept or reject what we are confronted with. So what would you like to have more of in your life - irritation, anger, resentment, disappointment - or peace, joy and contentment?

By now you've had time to adopt a new habit and when you find yourself confused, stressed or discouraged, you will be able to reduce it to a haiku and begin to see the perfection in imperfection whether in yourself or others. The next time you feel angry or frustrated, instead of counting to ten try composing a haiku in your head and see how it can alleviate those unwanted feelings.

One time-tested way to achieve peace and serenity in this hectic world is through the creative arts.

You probably know people who manage to get away from it all by becoming absorbed in painting, music or pottery. Not all of us can do this however – first of all we may feel that we lack the talent or discipline, and many of these pursuits also require a big investment in the way of time, space and equipment. The beauty of haiku is that anyone can do it anywhere, and the only equipment required is a pen and paper.

Haiku is the perfect tool to take you from wherever you are now to a place of serenity; a place where you can truly feel the perfection in each moment. You've now learned how to write good haiku easily and effortlessly. Once you get into the habit of doing this on a regular basis you will begin to notice your stress falling away.

As you begin dropping your judgements and living in the present, it will become easier and easier to achieve the serenity that can sometimes feel so elusive. It is simply a matter of changing the way you form your thoughts and that is something that anyone can do through the process of composing haiku. Changing the way you think even just a little bit, can make big changes in your life. This book will guide you through the steps that can change the way you will form your thoughts, and once you do that, you will be able to move through any situation with peace and tranquility. When your mind is at peace, you can and will feel every bit as tranquil as you would at the end of the pier – with no one between you and the water and nothing between you and the sky.

Made in the USA
Columbia, SC
18 March 2019